◨ READERS

Level 1

Level 2

A Note to Parents

DK READERS is a compelling program for beginning readers, designed in conjunction with leading literacy experts, including Dr. Linda Gambrell, Distinguished Professor of Education at Clemson University. Dr. Gambrell has served as President of the National Reading Conference, the College Reading Association, and the International Reading Association.

Beautiful illustrations and superb full-color photographs combine with engaging, easy-to-read stories to offer a fresh approach to each subject in the series. Each DK READER is guaranteed to capture a child's interest while developing his or her reading skills, general knowledge, and love of reading.

The five levels of DK READERS are aimed at different reading abilities, enabling you to choose the books that are exactly right for your child:

Pre-level 1: Learning to read
Level 1: Beginning to read
Level 2: Beginning to read alone
Level 3: Reading alone
Level 4: Proficient readers

The "normal" age at which a child begins to read can be anywhere from three to eight years old. Adult participation through the lower levels is very helpful for providing encouragement, discussing storylines, and sounding out unfamiliar words.

No matter which level you select, you can be sure that you are helping your child learn to read, then read to learn!

DK

LONDON, NEW YORK, MUNICH,
MELBOURNE, and DELHI

Editorial Assistant Ruth Amos
Senior Editor Hannah Dolan
Designer Richard Horsford
Jacket Designer Rhys Thomas
Pre-Production Producer Rebecca Fallowfield
Producer Danielle Smith
Managing Editor Laura Gilbert
Design Manager Maxine Pedliham
Art Director Ron Stobbart
Publishing Manager Julie Ferris
Publishing Director Simon Beecroft
Reading Consultant
Linda B. Gambrell, Ph.D.
Lucasfilm
Executive Editor J. W. Rinzler
Art Director Troy Alders
Keeper of the Holocron Leland Chee
Director of Publishing Carol Roeder
Rovio
Approvals Editor Nita Ukkonen
Senior Graphic Designer Jan Schulte-Tigges
Publishing and Licensing Manager
Laura Nevanlinna
Vice President of Book Publishing
Sanna Lukander

First published in the United States in 2013 by
DK Publishing
345 Hudson Street, New York, New York 10014
10 9 8 7 6 5 4 3 2 1
001-196556-Nov/13
Page design copyright © 2013 Dorling Kindersley Limited
Angry Birds™ & © 2009–2013 Rovio Entertainment Ltd.
All Rights Reserved.
© 2013 Lucasfilm Ltd. & ™. All rights reserved.
Used under authorization.

DK books are available at special discounts when purchased in bulk
for sales promotions, premiums, fund-raising, or educational use.
For details, contact:
DK Publishing Special Markets,
345 Hudson Street, New York, New York 10014
SpecialSales@dk.com

A catalog record for this book is available
from the Library of Congress.

ISBN: 978-1-4654-1537-0 (Paperback)
ISBN: 978-1-4654-1538-7 (Hardcover)

Color reproduction by Altaimage, UK
Printed and bound in China by L-Rex

Discover more at
www.dk.com
www.starwars.com

Contents

DK READERS

BEGINNING TO READ
1

ANGRY BIRDS
STAR WARS
II

DARTH SWINDLE'S SECRETS

Written by Scarlett O'Hara

Criminal mastermind

Who is that hiding under
a hood?

It is the evil Pig Lord
Darth Swindle!

He has lots of nasty secrets.

Evil
grin

Hidden weapon

Swindle wants
to rule the
galaxy and eat
all the candy
and junk food.

His snout is
good for smelling
out food.

snout

The Pork Side

A lot of pigs are on sneaky Swindle's side.
It is called the Pork Side.

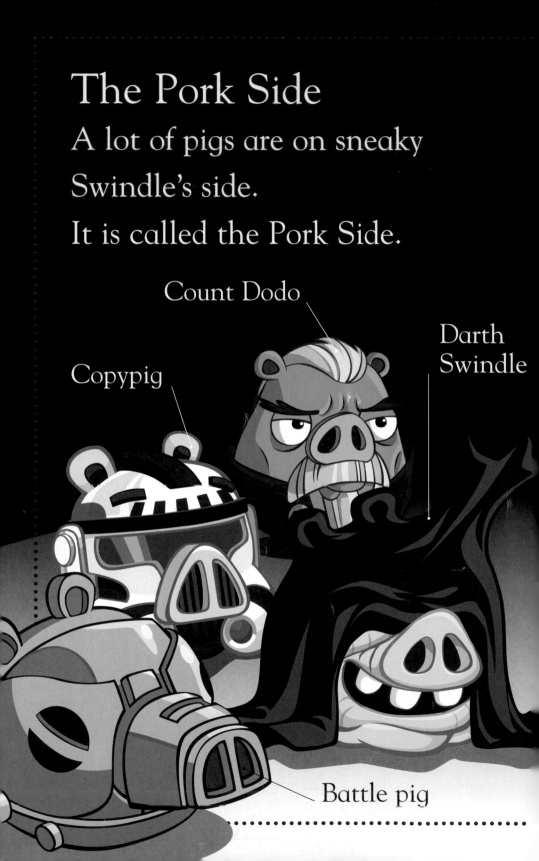

Count Dodo

Darth Swindle

Copypig

Battle pig

The pigs want to eat all
the junk food!
They also want to find The
Egg, which has the power
to rule the galaxy.

Warhog

Darth Moar

General
Grunter

Brave birds

Here are the good birds!
Some of the birds
are Jedi Bird warriors.
They are brave fighters.

C–3PYOLK

Moa Windu

Obi-Wan
Kaboomi

Quail-Gon

Only Yoda Bird knows where
to find The Egg.
It is disguised as R2-EGG2.
Don't tell Darth Swindle!

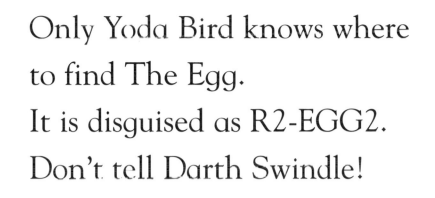

R2-EGG2

Queen Peckmé

Redkin
Skywalker

Jar Jar
Wings

Yoda Bird

Copypigs

Watch out! Darth Swindle
has an army of Copypigs.
He orders them to search the
galaxy for candy.

Wide
visor

The Copypigs are very stupid.
They do not understand
Swindle's greedy orders.
They copy one another
and get confused!

Piggy
ears

Sleek
gray hair

Snooty
face

Pig Lords

Darth Swindle commands
several pesky Pig Lords.

Count Dodo used to be a Jedi.
Now he is a horrible hog!

Fierce General Grunter's
body is made out of metal.
He fights with four lightsabers!

Lightsaber

Tough armor

Grunter's gang

General Grunter leads an
army of droids.

Battle pigs are not very bright
because their programming
went wrong!

droids

Long
snout

Twin
blasters

Glowing eye

The Warhogs are very fast and
have lots of weapons.
Everybody is scared of
them—even the Jedi Birds.

Frightened fowl

Goofy Jar Jar Wings and loyal Terebacca are in big trouble!

Furry feathers

Tough metal shell

Eyes on stalks

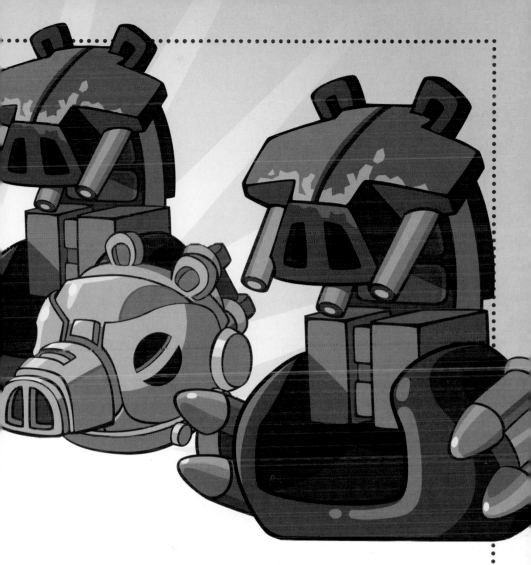

Darth Swindle thinks they
have hidden food from him.

Swindle sends in his droids
to teach them a lesson.

Jedi enemies

Darth Swindle has many enemies.
One enemy is the Jedi Bird Moa Windu.

Glowing lightsaber

Bushy brow

Moa is a great lightsaber fighter.

The wise Jedi Yoda Bird
and Moa talk together.
How can they stop Swindle?

Wise wrinkled
forehead

Dark pig power

Darth Swindle challenges Moa to a duel. Sly Swindle wants to defeat Moa and rule the roost!

Pow! Swindle
zaps Moa with his
Force lightning.

Force
lightning

The wicked pig wins the fight.

Jedi cloak

Bounty hunters

Darth Swindle sends these bounty hunters to capture enemy birds.

Zam Weasel uses electro-goggles to find her target.

Zam's electro-goggles

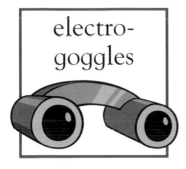

electro-
goggles

Cunning Jango
Fatt uses a
jetpack to escape
from trouble.

Jango's jetpack

Crazy warrior

Watch out for this crazy pig!
His name is Darth Moar.

He is Darth Swindle's
pig apprentice.

Head
horn

Evil
grin

Moar joined the Pork Side
when he was young.

Swindle tempted him
with lots of junk food.

Staring
eyes

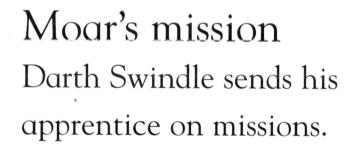

Moar's mission

Darth Swindle sends his apprentice on missions.

double-bladed lightsaber

Moar has a double-bladed lightsaber.

Look! Darth Moar is trying
to capture Queen Peckmé.

Quail-Gon and Obi-Wan
try to stop him.

Powerful
blade

Green bird
lightsaber

Sharp beak

Battle scar

Tempting trick

Darth Swindle is
a very sly pig.
He tries to tempt
Jedi Birds over to
the Pork Side.

Swindle tempts Redkin
Skywalker to join the pigs.

Redkin becomes the Pig
Lord Lard Vader.

Huge
helmet

Watch out for the birds!

These birds won't let
Darth Swindle win.
They will fight back.

They will work together
to beat the evil Pork Side.
They will stop the pigs from
finding The Egg...

Glossary

Double-bladed lightsaber

A weapon with a beam of energy at each end.

Droids

A type of robot, like battle pigs or Warhogs.

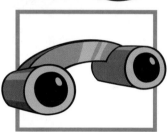

Electro-goggles

Goggles used to spy on a person or thing.

Force lightning

A deadly power that only Pig Lords use.

Snout

A round, flat nose that some animals have.

Index